MW01290932

IGNITE THE FLAME

A Leader's Devotion

LOGAN RAGAN

WESTBOW
PRESS®
A DIVISION OF THOMAS NELSON
& ZONDERVAN

WestBow Press books may be ordered through booksellers or by contacting:

WestBow Press
A Division of Thomas Nelson & Zondervan
1663 Liberty Drive
Bloomington, IN 47403
www.westbowpress.com
844-714-3454

ISBN: 978-1-6642-3242-6 (sc)
ISBN: 978-1-6642-3244-0 (hc)
ISBN: 978-1-6642-3243-3 (e)

Library of Congress Control Number: 2021908362

Print information available on the last page.

WestBow Press rev. date: 04/30/2021

ENDORSEMENTS

We all encounter things in our lives that hinder our growth. They stop us from reaching our true potential and can often hinder and hurt those around us. We all wish we were further along than where we are, but this only comes as we bravely face the things, we are afraid to face. This devotional will help you prayerfully face things that you might have always been afraid to face. What if in 30 days you could begin to experience slow, gentle courage birthed in your heart directly from God? God desires to connect with you and strengthen you. Spend time with this helpful book.

-

David Fischer
Church Planter, Birmingham, AL

This is a must-read primer for anyone beginning or reaffirming their journey with Jesus Christ. Once you begin, you will be enticed to immerse yourself into the entire book. Yet, I would challenge you to experience these bite-sized gifts as they were intended, as daily foundational truths that will stay with you step for step as you gain traction on the path towards your destiny.

-

Brian T Church
CEO and Best-Selling Author

For young people especially, our digital Information Age causes hyper distraction making it hard to slow down to focus on what is important. Thankfully, this excellent devotional was written by a young man *while* he was young and beginning the slow, difficult work of focusing on the most important things of life. This book is a great exit ramp to living a life of purpose no matter the age.

-

Dr. Delvin Pikes, DMin
Nashville Campus Director, Every Nation Campus

This book shares an incredible journey that highlights the real-world trials we all face in our everyday lives. This inspiring read will help you recognize the customized path that God has laid out for each of his followers. As followers of Christ, we are leaders in society. *Ignite the Flame* encourages all of us to apply our gift of leadership by providing practical ways to practice holding faith in all of our life endeavors. It is with pleasure that I highly encourage all to read and reflect on this writing.

-

Dr. Ming Wang, Harvard & MIT (MD, magna cum laude); PhD (laser physics)
CEO, Aier-USA

Many Christians start their journey without knowing what the next steps are. *Ignite the Flame* provides a solution for this. It provides practical steps for addressing real-life issues that we all face. After reading this book, you will be equipped with how to handle difficult life issues and be well on your way to building a solid foundation in Christ.

-

Addison Tweedy
Director, God's Not Dead Events

While in college, there are many distractions pulling students' attention. Many of these diversions keep them from addressing the root cause of the issues they may be facing. This book offers great, quick, practical applications for dealing with those issues. *Ignite the Flame* really helps in recentering what is important in life.

-

Nick Jones
North American Director, Every Nation Campus

Life can get hard and at times it can be difficult to identify what's causing it. However, the one thing we can control is how we respond, but that can even be challenging. At times, we might need a catalyst in our life to get us moving again. This book helps identify areas in our character that may impact our view on life. I encourage all to take the time to go through this book and after 30 days, you should have a changed perspective on life.

-

JT McCraw
Executive Pastor, Bethel World Outreach Center Church

I would like to dedicate this book to my grandmother, the sweetest lady I know. She encouraged me to take a step out of my comfort zone and to try and help others with my words.

CONTENTS

FOREWORD

It's been an honor to get to know Logan Ragan, a dedicated and motivated disciple of Jesus. I have watched him seek God, develop a partnership team, get married, and undergo brain surgery — no small matter. Logan is an overcomer.

Ignite the Flame, is an offering of Logan's overcoming heart. He's focused on the private and hidden journey that we as Christ-followers, must have with God. It is both a prayer and a devotional to join with God, to get to know Him, and lean into His accepting and always-loving presence.

Mapmakers for centuries have used the four points of a compass to guide travelers. In order for a compass, and then the map, to work as a legitimate guide, it must first establish "true north."

As Christ-followers, our "true north" is defined by the calling of God and His leading in our lives. Logan invites us to this "true north." In Deuteronomy 2:3, Moses instructed the Israelites to stop doing laps around the mountain and "turn north." This command was more than geography, it was their way into the promised land.

It takes courage, faith, and obedience to enter your promise and "promised land," whatever that may be. The direction on how to get there, is your "true north."

Whether you are turning to God for the first time or returning to God once again, both require devotion. This simple book in your hands has the power to help your devotional life. As we devote ourselves to Christ we are headed north and will undoubtedly receive the promises of God and be transformed by his grace.

May God speak to you and draw close to you.

All the best,

Ron Lewis
Sr. Minister, Every Nation NYC

PREFACE

A s I was growing up, I had many ambitions. However, at some point in my life, this world took its toll on me. I began to accept lies about myself, lies that the world would say are normal. I was letting people define who I am and where my worth came from. I should have let God do that.

Having a firm understanding about God and how Jesus's life impacts my life truly helped me get through troubling times in my life. Faith mixed with knowledge and understanding can help you through many situations. As I began to comprehend more about my faith, I noticed my ambitions, goals, and hope for life started to come back. Except this time, my goals and ambitions were not about what I wanted to achieve but what God wanted to achieve through me.

This devotional is compiled with many of my thoughts during low times in my life. As I poured my heart out to God, He was faithful to respond, and I captured what I felt the Holy Spirit was ministering to me. This would at times come through the form of a song I knew, sermons, and the Bible. God gave me encouragement during my darkest times, and it made me realize how He has called us all to be leaders. My hope and prayer are that this book encourages everyone to see that they are called to be leaders in Christ, how to be a people group set apart from the rest of the world, and how to deal with daily struggles we all have.

This book is comprised of thirty devotions meant to be read once a day, and the scripture should be read as the reader reads the devotion. As the scripture is read, stop and think how that scripture and that part of the devotion can be applied to your life or to others. Remember, you are loved by God for no other reason than for being yourself. In Christ, you are a leader, and your current situation in life does not define you. God defines you and has blessings for you at every point in your life.

ACKNOWLEDGMENTS

I have to start by giving a special thanks to my amazing wife, Jocelyn, who gave me tremendous help and support during the writing process. Every section I wrote, she was more than happy to read over it and give encouraging feedback.

Thanks to Jason for walking with me during some of my hardest times. He helped me understand how to apply my faith during low times. I am glad that God placed you in my life.

Thanks to Jerry for being a positive influence on my decision to start vocational ministry. I'm not sure this book would be published if I did not go into ministry.

Thanks to Leo, who has helped me deepen my faith in Christ. While, at the same time, speaking positive encouragement over my life and helping me navigate various situations in my life.

Thanks to my family for giving me the motivational support needed as I wrote this book.

Obtaining Peace

The church, the physical place where we gather to worship, has failed the Church, the collective individuals who believe Jesus is Lord and Savior. The church only offers peace; it is a place where the Church comes to feel good and only gains momentary peace. The church should be teaching the believers of Christ how to gain the supernatural peace that only comes from God and that will never leave (2 Thessalonians 3:16). This peace is obtained through worship, prayer, and reading God's Word, the Bible. Through worship, you give praise to the One who created you. By praying, you rely on Jesus to comfort and give you peace (Psalms 29:11; 32:7; 85:8). When you do this, you are casting your burdens onto Him (Psalms 55:22; Matthew 11:28–30; 1 Peter 5:7). When you read God's Word and store it in your heart, you will be able to use it during challenging times (Psalms 119:9–11; 1:1–2).

Challenging times could be literally anything. It could be when you mess up by saying or doing something you should not. When this happens, the devil likes to come in and trash-talk you, saying things like, "How are you, a Christian, doing and talking like this? You are not true to your God. You are not a real Christian. You may as well not try because you will never be perfect."

When the devil attacks your mind like this, you *must* take your thoughts captive according to 2 Corinthians 10:5. However, when you let these thoughts run rampant, they will consume you, and there will be no peace in you. When you feel like there's no peace in your soul, it's difficult to focus on Jesus and be useful to others around you. Like Peter on the water, when the waves were rough and the wind tumultuous, he lost his focus on Jesus and fell deep into the waters (Matthew 14:25–33). That is humanity when we are not living and walking in the peace that Jesus so graciously promised.

Ensure you obtain peace by taking your thoughts captive, worshipping, praying, and reading God's Word.

Prayer

Lord, thank You for providing ways for me to connect with You. Thank You for Your Word that teaches me I can do all things through You. Father, I ask that You help teach and remind me to take my thoughts captive and to keep my focus on You. Through Your teachings, I ask that You give me a supernatural peace that will never leave. I pray this all in Jesus's name. Amen.

Application & Reflection

What did you learn from this lesson? How can you apply it to your life and others?

_____

_____

_____

_____

MAKING DECISIONS

D o not make decisions while mad or angered. It is also never a good idea to react out of anger (James 1:19–21). If a thought is acted on while angered, you create an opportunity to hurt or damage a relationship or someone's soul. Proverbs 29:11 says that the wise will bring calm in the end, and if you do not know what to do in the moment, then pray.

Human anger will never produce the righteousness God wishes for each us to live out (James 1:19–20). This human anger may take place when we feel like we are being ignored. Or we become hurt in some form and lash out. However, human anger is different from righteous anger, which is when we see something evil taking place that harms someone. This type of anger does not give way to sin.

Nonetheless, all things must be submitted unto Christ. To produce the righteousness that God desires, though, you must first repent and get rid of all moral filth in your life (James 1:21; Acts 3:19). You do this by humbling yourself, accepting that you are wrong, and receiving God's Word that has been spoken into your life.

Never draw a conclusion from what you can see or cannot see. For unless you fully know what is going on, what you do know is just temporary and subject to change (2 Corinthians 4:18). You must pray for wisdom and discernment so that you may critically analyze a situation to apply the knowledge you have concerning that situation. But even after that, it is wise to give it to God (Proverbs 3:5–6). Even if you have consulted your worldly friends on something, you should never make a decision based on what they say or what other people are doing. Always refer to the Bible, pray, and seek godly counsel (Psalm 37:30–1; Proverbs 11:14).

Prayer

Heavenly Father, thank You for giving me gifts graciously and for Your never-ending mercy. You are the Lord over my life, and I will always seek Your ways for Your ways are higher than my ways. Lord, I ask that You guide my footsteps, give me enough light to see the next step in front of me, and let my faith in You grow. I humbly ask that You reveal the mysteries of this earth to me, and give me the wisdom and understanding of how to always walk in righteousness and how to make righteous decisions. I pray this all in Jesus's name. Amen.

Application & Reflection

What did you learn from this lesson? How can you apply it to your life and others?

_____

_____

_____

_____

My Rock

Have you ever felt like you are treated differently (not in a good way) and especially since accepting Jesus as your Lord and Savior? Have you ever wondered why there may be conflict in your own household or constant afflictions in your life? It is because as Christians we are set apart (1 Peter 2:9). We are not like those who have not died to their flesh or their own desires and pleasures. This is why we Christians do not fit in with the rest of the world (John 15:19). For we do not battle flesh and blood, but we go to battle in the supernatural—spiritual— warfare (Ephesians 6:12). Knowing this, be aware that it may even seem like your family is turning against you (Psalm 27:10).

However, Deuteronomy 31:6 says that no matter where you may go in life or what may come against you, He will never leave you or forsake you. God does not start something and then not finish it or see it through (Philippians 1:6). His love never fails, never gives up, and never runs out. No matter how hard you push against Him, Jesus will be right there waiting for you. All you have to do is turn around. He is already there waiting for you with open arms.

You may feel alone, empty, and unwanted. But you are so much more than what people say you are. Look to Him for power and love, and you will have someone there when there is no one to turn to.

Never base a decision on your own understanding (Proverbs 3:5–6). Always pray before doing anything. Ask God to calm your soul, and to help you to discern His voice. Listen for the voice of God. Afterward, chase after God and His goodness so that you may do His will, not your will.

Prayer

Jesus, thank You for all the love and mercy You show me. You are my fortress, strong tower, and my rock. I thank You for always looking after me and for always having my back. Father, give me peace as troubles come my way. Teach me how to root my confidence in You and not in myself. And not letting it be found in other people's acceptance of me. I ask that You place mature Christians in my life who will give me encouragement during difficult times. I pray this all in Jesus's name. Amen.

Application & Reflection

What did you learn from this lesson? How can you apply it to your life and others?

_____

_____

_____

_____

THE ONLY CONSTANT
IN LIFE IS CHANGE

O ver time it seems that our hearts begin to harden, and we become insensitive. We allow for various things in our lives to shape and mold our perspectives on life instead of allowing an experiential relationship with Jesus and God's Holy Word to shape us. As time goes by, do we become resistant to change in our lives? What is stopping God from changing our hearts?

You cannot receive what God has planned for you while you are still trying to take control of your life. God's gift for you will stay outside your life, waiting for you to change. Like an onion that has many layers, you must peel away all the protective layers that have been built up as a defense (Jeremiah 24:7). With all these layers or defenses, you have created a barrier between you and God. Like a defeated king, you must surrender yourself and your kingdom—your will and life—so that you may become one with God (1 Corinthians 6:17).

This world and culture are always changing. Those who do not adapt to change, change that produces righteousness, get left behind. When change is the product of God's plan, it is good. But when change is the product of your own plan, it generally brings trouble (2 Peter 3:9). Change can sometimes be difficult to accept, but you must move on. By not accepting change, you could miss God's blessings.

When you stay in the same old rut or routine for so long, God will start to stir things up in your life (Isaiah 43:19). He does this to get you ready for something better. Change often comes not how we want it but how God wants it. Everything God gives us is a gift (James 1:17). However, just like a physical gift, we sometimes reject the gift God gives us simply because we have preconceived notions on what the gift should be based on the size, appearance, or what we want. Doesn't that sound prideful? We must change and receive every gift with joy and thanksgiving (1 Thessalonians 5:16–18).

Remember that God is consistent; He will never change (Malachi 3:6; Hebrews 13:8). Since God is constant with what He says and does, then it would be unwise to dismiss anything that God could be using to direct your life. When presented with challenges or change, be careful not to say, "This is not God." However, be encouraged to pray about it and submit it to the Holy Spirit (Job 22:21–22). Always seek Him.

When you are going through what feels like anguish and cannot understand what is going on, remember this: God is with you and is in the center of every challenge. His ways are the same today as they were yesterday (Numbers 23:19; Psalm 119:89), and when you feel like you will never see the light again, keep in mind that something is about to change.

Prayer

Jesus, thank You for all the blessings and favor You have given me. Thank You for even the smallest of blessings, like being able to see a beautiful sunset. In becoming a Christian, we are called to abandon our old ways, and I am thankful that You have empowered me to do so. I ask that the Holy Spirit gives me patience during times of change. Remind me to give thanks in all situations. I pray this all in Jesus's name. Amen.

Application & Reflection

What did you learn from this lesson? How can you apply it to your life and others?

_____

_____

_____

_____

NOT MY UNDERSTANDING

"Trust in the Lord with all your heart and lean not
on your own understanding; in all your ways submit
to him, and he will make your paths straight."
(Proverbs 3:5–6)

How many times have you tried to do something or make a decision based on your own understanding? This is such a humbling passage. God reminds us all that we will never survive this Christian walk if we rely on ourselves. If you try to accomplish something without Him, your path will surely become crooked and misguided (Psalm 118:8). With everything that we do, we must submit to His Lordship and His ways, not our ways.

If you feel confused, develop mixed feelings, or become unsure of a thought God has given you, remember this verse and pray to God. Ask for guidance, knowledge, a sound mind, and understanding of what the truth is and what is a lie from the devil (1 John 4:1). However, for you to clearly hear God and not mistake His voice for another's, you must be at peace and walk in peace. Peace as in your soul is not disturbed and anxious. This is accomplished by being doers of the Word and not just hearers of the Word (James 1:19–27).

People are always looking for answers. During times when you are looking for answers, you must remember to call out to God every day for advice instead of going to culture for help and guidance because God is the guidance that is above all other guidance

(Jeremiah 33:3; John 16:13). In many circumstances, we will grow weak and weary, but do not doubt your faith. Even if it feels like your soul is in a pit, never stop trusting God (Psalm 143:7–8). Know that God always has you where He wants you.

Prayer

God, I thank You for what You have blessed me with. I thank You for giving me every battle that comes my way for I shall use it to strengthen my faith in You. Help me to lean not on not my own understanding but on Your understanding. Give me the wisdom to help me make the decision You want me to make. I ask that every morning will bring me a closer understanding of Your unfailing love. Let me be a light shining in this dark world so that I may live like You, Jesus. I pray this all in Jesus's name. Amen.

Application & Reflection

What did you learn from this lesson? How can you apply it to your life and others?

_____

_____

_____

_____

DYING TO YOUR DESIRES

I f we are a new creation in Christ (2 Corinthians 5:17), then why does it seem so hard to allow God to do amazing works through us? The Bible makes it very clear that we have to abandon our old ways of life. In fact, it states that to save our lives, we must first lose them (Mark 8:35). To be able to be a new creation in Christ there are a few things that must take place. We must repent from our sins and believe that Jesus is our Lord and Savior (Luke 5:32; 24:46–47; Romans 10:9). Then, as completion of our belief in Christ and submission to His Lordship, we are to be water baptized (Matthew 28:19; Mark 16:16; 1 Peter 3:21; Acts 2:38; Romans 6:4). Then we will receive the gift of the Holy Spirit.

After having a supernatural change in your heart, one thing is certain: You must die to yourself, denying your fleshly desire, and pick up your cross daily (Luke 9:23). This means you must put aside your selfish desires daily and shoulder whatever challenges come your way by relying on the Holy Spirit to empower you to do so. This is all relevant because if you were still indulging in your old ways, how could God possibly get the glory when people examine your life? You would just be considered a "nice" person. Will you fail at times? Sure. We all do. But when you fail, and the Holy Spirit reveals sin in your life, you must fall on Jesus and rely on His strength to get you up (Psalm 37:23–24; 1 John 1:9). You must ask Jesus to heal you from any emotional pain that sin may have caused, and ask God to replace it with a blessing (Philippians 4:6).

So you must get rid of your selfish desires so that God may work in you. Or better yet, use you to help someone else. Think about it. If you do not die to your desires and let God work in and through you, others may miss their blessings. Therefore, go out today trying to let God lead you. Take a step back, and see what miracles He has planned for you.

Prayer

Lord, You are worthy, glorious, and deserving of all praise. I thank You for all the blessings and provisions You have given me. Thank You for not letting anything stop You from showing me grace. Father, bring my heart to the cross, where Your love poured out for me. I lay my life down for You and ask that You rid me of myself because I ultimately belong to You. Lead me to Your love and to live life as You did, Jesus. I pray this all in Jesus's name. Amen.

Application & Reflection

What did you learn from this lesson? How can you apply it to your life and others?

_____

_____

_____

_____

WHERE IS YOUR
HAPPINESS FOUND?

Have you ever felt hopeless about something? Have you ever asked yourself, "Where are You, God?" It is easy to plague yourself with questions like that, and those questions can plunge you into a dark and lonely place. It seems questions like this arise most often when you have everything but still feel empty, are not fully reliant on God, or when you lose everything you believe you need. This can be a loss of a job, a child, your house, or anything for that matter. Just read the book of Job. He was a faithful individual, yet he lost everything. Although he lost everything, in the end he gained more than he ever had before, and his faith grew.

You, a strong-willed person, may say, "If I could just do better, I will get out of this rut and bad situation." But you cannot! Apart from God, you cannot do better at filling the emptiness inside (Jeremiah 17:5–8). You must rely on God; He will help you through all situations (Proverbs 3:5). You may have experienced happiness while being successful and living a comfortable life. However, are you experiencing happiness when your life is crumbling around you? The only true happiness you will ever experience is while you are fully relying on God, seeking after His face and not His hand (Jeremiah 29:12–14).

Throughout the Bible, God is saying to you, "just let Me love and help you" (Philippians 4:19). It is clear that God hears you and will answer you when you diligently seek after Him (Proverbs 8:17). This requires quality time or encounters with Him, not just a lot of empty-hearted prayers. Meaning, are you having adequate time to talk—pray—to Him, give Him glory, praise, and worship? And are you listening to what He says by reading the Bible? It is all in the motives of the heart. God judges the heart and knows when the time spent with Him is in relationship with Him (Psalm 44:21).

Keep in mind you are not the only one who has ever had challenging times. In fact, there has been a human who has dealt with every kind of loss, sadness, opposition, and difficulty. Jesus went through many of the same things that you may face in today's time (Hebrews 4:14–15). What better person to relate to than Jesus? Jesus is God's answer to every question. Chase after a relationship with Jesus to find fulfillment (John 14:6).

Stay hopeful in every challenge. You are in the right place if you're being rebuked, persecuted, and rejected for your faith and belief (1 Peter 4:12–14; Matthew 5:11). In times like that, you will truly know what it means to rely on God to comfort you, and out of that situation, you and your faith will grow stronger.

Prayer

Good and gracious Father, You are my Rock and fortress. You deliver me from my enemies' hands. Thank You, Lord, for always being there for me, even when I am not wanting to spend time with You. Show me areas in my life that need to be refined, areas that are causing me to not pursue You during times of good and bad. You are ultimately my vision and guide in this life, so Lord, help me to always lean on You and diligently seek You. I pray this all in Jesus's name. Amen.

Application & Reflection

What did you learn from this lesson? How can you apply it to your life and others?

_____

_____

_____

_____

FORGIVENESS

Have you ever had an argument with someone or felt like someone has wronged you? Sure you have; we all have. It seems it is a part of life. But they are also opportunities for you to show God's grace (Colossians 4:6 AMP). Nonetheless, how many times have you let the argument go too far and then you and the other person do not talk for a few days? This allows for bitterness to set in, and now there is a greater chance for the problem never to be resolved because pride is more than likely in the mix. Who likes to admit they are wrong?

The Bible teaches that if we do not forgive others, God in heaven will not forgive us (Matthew 6:14–15). In addition to forgiving others because it is commanded, when you forgive others it helps set you free. When you do not forgive, you are allowing this person to have control over your life by having pent-up hurt follow you. Instead of allowing the pain of unforgiveness follow you, live in peace with everyone and show grace. If you do not, how will others see the Lord (Hebrews 12:14–15 NASB)? How many people do you just "write off" when you become angry or are hurt by them? Instead of turning people away, accept them with unconditional kindness (Ephesians 4:29–32).

What do most people do with hurt or trauma? Typically, the deeper the hurt or trauma, the better you try to make yourself look on the outside. You may put on a mask to try to hide your pain because you want to be accepted or perhaps for another reason. Thus, you put on this mask and keep living life as nothing has happened. Until one day, the mask seems to be a part of who you are. When you do this, you are just pushing that guilt, shame, and pain deeper inside you, which hurts you more (Psalm 32:3–5; Proverbs 28:13). If you spend most of your time fixing up your outside but never taking the time to truly fix or address what is going on with your soul, you will still have feelings of misery or emptiness. Only Jesus can set your soul free from a cycle of shame, fear, and control (John 8:31–36).

How can you tell if you have truly forgiven your neighbor? If you can, in some way bless your neighbor and pray blessings over him or her, then you have truly forgiven the person. For how can anyone show love with hatred in their hearts (1 John 2:9–10)?

Prayer

Lord, thank You for sacrificing Yourself and for being a perfect example of how to forgive your enemies. Father, forgiving my enemies is very hard. I want to get revenge on the wrong done to me, but I know You are the One who takes care of this. Help me not to indulge my flesh, and let me humbly serve my enemies in love. Let me live out how You treated Your enemies with love, compassion, and grace. I ask that You give me opportunities to show love to my enemies so that my faith may grow in You, and that You may use me in greater capacities. I pray this all in Jesus's name. Amen.

Application & Reflection

What did you learn from this lesson? How can you apply it to your life and others?

_____

_____

_____

_____

THE HARD DAYS

You may often be told how wonderful it is being a Christian. And it is! However, rarely does anyone tell you about the hard days. These days typically follow experiencing something wonderful from God. You may feel alone, depressed, hopeless, and that you will never experience God's goodness again. Know that He has never and will never leave you (Isaiah 41:10). During these hard days, find at least one thing a day to be thankful for (1 Thessalonians 5:16–18).

Keep in mind, once the pleasures of this world pass by, this life has only pain and emptiness left to offer (1 John 2:15–17). If you feel alone, that no one is with you on this journey, forget that God is with you, or feel abandoned by Him, remember to tell yourself that He would never leave His child alone (Psalm 94:14).

The devil is a punk and will kick you while you are down, and even push you into a deeper hole if you let him (1 Peter 5:8). The devil, also known as the enemy, will remind you of times when your life was so great before your current situation, and he will always mask it with saying something like, "Look how you were able to do all these things. Now look. You are relying on God, and look where that got you." Take these thoughts captive, or the enemy will have a foothold in your life (2 Corinthians 10:5). Keep in mind the devil only comes to steal, kill, and destroy everything (John 10:10).

The Lord, our God, is always for us and never against us (Romans 8:31). He will never forsake you in your weaknesses, but during trials and tribulations, He will build our faith (Romans 5:3–5; Isaiah

41:10). You overcome these hard days by being thankful even in suffering and leaning on God for strength. You can rebuild your strength through Him by prayer, worship, and reading His Word (Colossians 4:2). In all things, let His peace flow through your heart. You do this by casting your burdens onto Him (Colossians 3:15–17).

Prayer

Father, I thank You for all that You do in my life. Sometimes my life seems futile, my heart aches, and I want to just lie down and quit. It is then when I cry out to You most for I know You are about to tear down a wall, and I will never have to look back. So I ask once more, show me Your grace. I give this pain and burden to You. I know You'll never forsake me. Teach me how to walk in Your peace, and give me a hunger and a passion for Your Word. I pray this all in Jesus's name. Amen.

Application & Reflection

What did you learn from this lesson? How can you apply it to your life and others?

_____

_____

_____

_____

LETTING GO

How strong do you think you are? No, not physically, but spiritually. What even makes you spiritually strong? Spiritual strength is not determined by how much you can do on your own accord. It definitely is not measured by how well you can provide for yourself. In fact, the Bible says God will give strength to those who are weary (Isaiah 40:29). So much so, that as you hope in the Lord, He shall renew your strength (Isaiah 40:31)!

Regarding past hurts, true strength does not lie with what you can hold on to; it lies in what you can release. What sense does it make to hold purposely onto pain or not address the pain by not going to God for help? Hurtful places are really growing places if you allow them to be. Moreover, Jesus says that if you want to be His disciple, you must take up your cross and follow Him (Matthew 16:24). What could be more painful than carrying a cross, an item that was used for torture? This is a metaphor Jesus used, but walking with Him is not easy.

Through times of hurt, God might be trying to shake something loose in your life (James 1:2–4). Be careful not to let it destroy you, and never become angry to the point of sinning or have unforgiveness with that situation (Ephesians 4:26–27). You have no right to walk in unforgiveness, and you should be slow to become angry at the situation that caused the hurt (Proverbs 16:32; 17:9). Human anger does not produce righteousness (James 1:19–21). When you try to retaliate to hurt and pain in the same nature, it will ultimately destroy you spiritually (1 John 3:14–15). What you do out of retaliation will essentially build walls, thinking it will protect you, but really it is what is holding you back.

When you carry around past hurts instead of letting God really heal you, you make the people in your life pay for the hurt that occurred to you (Ephesians 4:31). That unhealed hurt can change you in many ways, and thus result in a pattern of hurting others. Regarding the people who hurt you, it is not about the hurt done by them; it is about the way you handle the situation (Proverbs 19:11). When that pain and anger says that you are entitled to act any way you wish, be that strong person the Holy Spirit empowers you to be and let go. Allow God to heal you.

Forgiveness is often seen as unlocking a door to let someone free. But in all actuality, it is not the one who caused the hurt you set free, but it is yourself who is being set free from bondage (Isaiah 43:18–21). When you start not to feel free, look back and see what burdens you are carrying. You will never experience true freedom if you do not learn how to forgive and let go of the past (Matthew 6:14–15).

Prayer

Heavenly Father, You are holy, righteous, good, and mighty. You are always good to me, and I thank You for that. Thank You for always loving me and never holding anything back from me. Sometimes, God, it is hard to let go of situations, especially the ones that hurt and have caused pain. Teach me how to let go and let You take control of situations. Give me the courage to pick up my cross daily and to die to my fleshly desires daily. Help me be humble so that You may have complete control of my life and that I may fall under Your Lordship. Thank You, Jesus, for bearing my sins and allowing me to walk in Your peace. I pray this all in Jesus's name. Amen.

Application & Reflection

What did you learn from this lesson? How can you apply it to your life and others?

_____

_____

_____

_____

HANDLING IRRITATIONS

Have you ever found yourself replying sharply or harshly to someone? Have you ever stopped to consider what the root reason is for responding like that? When this happens, it is a good time to examine yourself. Reflect to see how your relationship is with God. Are you staying in His Word, are you encouraging others, are you being thankful for all things, and so on?

Typically, when an individual irritates you to the point of speaking harshly to the person, you may try to avoid him or her. What if almost everyone around you begins to irritate you? This world will tell you to isolate yourself to avoid those situations because you do not need their negativity in your life. However, Jesus has called us to greater things than just to be alone. He tells us to make disciples of all nations, but you cannot do that if you are off to yourself (Matthew 28:19–20). You may say that you have tried to be around others, and you keep getting hurt, or it just does not work out. If God has truly put you in a season of dedication to Him, you will never really be alone because He always provides a support group—the Church, the body of believers (Romans 12:6; Galatians 6:2; 1 John 1:7).

We must never rely on the advice of those who are not under Jesus's Lordship. For their intentions and guidance may have our best interests in mind, but ultimately, their hearts are wickedly deceitful and can cause confusion when comparing their advice to God's advice (Matthew 15:17–19; Jeremiah 14:9). If you find yourself agreeing and turning to them for advice more than the Bible, something is out of alignment in your spiritual life. For if you are saved, you are a new creation in Christ and have access to an infinite amount of wisdom (2 Corinthians 5:17–18). If you do find yourself being propped up by culture more than by God, retreat to God. Submit all requests to Him, and be thankful for all He does in your life (Philippians 4:4–7).

Even if you are walking in obedience in Christ and not accepting advice from the world, you must still be careful not to become self-righteous (Galatians 2:16). You have to keep in mind that you were once a part of this crowd (Ephesians 2:1–10). You, too, were once uninformed of what to do. So do not look down on anyone; be the light needed in a dark place. Treat them as Jesus treated you when you became saved. Simply love God and love people.

Prayer

Thank You, Lord, for all Your blessings. Thank You for always comforting me and for always giving me a support group. Help me see how the support group can help me. I ask that the Holy Spirit give me wisdom on how to handle situations when I become irritated and that You will reveal the darkest parts of my heart. I want to know what is holding me back from loving others as You love them. Help me keep my pride in check and never to feel as though I am better than the next person. I pray this all in Jesus's name. Amen.

Application & Reflection

What did you learn from this lesson? How can you apply it to your life and others?

_____

_____

_____

_____

HUMBLE BEGINNINGS

N ot many people are born into fame and wealth. However, when you have a humble beginning, you will typically do either one of two things. When you become successful, you might become prideful and say you made it out and did it all yourself. Or you might humble yourself and thank God for everything you have accomplished. To be humble is to have or show a modest or low estimate of one's importance, which is exactly what God calls us to be (Ephesians 4:1–3).

When you examine humanity in comparison to Jesus, why are humans able to live so freely and easily on this earth? Yes, Jesus died so that you and I may be able to, but think about it. Jesus was beaten, whipped, humiliated, and killed (Luke 22:63). All of this was done just so you could live a better life. Because of Jesus's example of humility and His divine power giving everything you need for a godly life, you are able to live life joyfully with a humble attitude (2 Peter 1:3–4).

Due to your past sins, you do not deserve this life. If anything, you, instead of Jesus, should have had to suffer for your sins. However, that is what makes God so amazing. He loves you so much that He sent His own Son to pay the price of sin for you (John 3:16–18). God did this because He always wanted humanity to be in a close relationship with Him. So remember, you are always worthy of God's grace because Jesus died as a sacrifice for all your sins. By God's grace, you are what you are (1 Corinthians 15:10).

Although Paul is referring to his own apostleship in this verse, you are in God what He has called you to be, and no one can take that away from you.

Remain humble in God when going through this life (1 Peter 5:6–7). None of this, what you have, is your own. It all belongs to Him (Job 1:21; Psalm 24:1). Never do anything to gain for yourself; instead, do it to please God (Proverbs 1:19). Always thank God for the things and people in your life for they can be taken away in an instant. When you start to succeed, don't forget who allowed you to get there (Proverbs 16:3). Jesus humbled Himself so that we might be in relationship with God, so the least we can do is give thanks and be humbled before Him.

Prayer

Heavenly Father, You are truly great and deserve all praise. I thank You for the air in my lungs and the air that I breathe. Lord, being humbled never feels good, but when I align myself with Your Word, I know it will strengthen me. So Father, remove all my pride; break me apart from my earthly desires. I am Yours and surrender my life to You. As I am exalted by You, I ask that you keep me humble and grateful for how far You have brought me from where my journey began. I pray this all in Jesus's name. Amen.

Application & Reflection

What did you learn from this lesson? How can you apply it to your life and others?

_____

_____

_____

_____

A LIFE UNDESERVED

Have you ever sinned? Of course you have; you are human. Sinning disqualifies you from entering the kingdom of heaven, but thank God He allows you to be redeemed and showed you mercy (Ephesians 2:4–5). In fact, God became man in Jesus Christ, died for your sins, and was then raised to life for your justification (Romans 4:25). So He died and shed innocent blood, which covers and is payment for all your sins. Then He was resurrected from the grave to justify you so that you may be in right standing with God. If God humbles Himself this much, how much more are you to humble yourself? But praise God for all this because you are fearfully and wonderfully made (Psalm 139:14)!

Have you ever imagined God celebrating you? Just picture God in heaven, rejoicing and smiling at you. Think about that. He is rejoicing over a creation that rejects Him and is so morally unclean in the comparison of a holy God (Isaiah 64:6; Romans 3:23–24). Just because you are inherently undeserving of His grace does not mean He does not give it to you as a gift—something that is unearned, grace (Ephesians 2:8). This should let you know how much He truly loves you. If everyone seems like they hate you or dislike you for what you have done, just remember God is still there, smiling at you. This is seen through all His promises and blessings (Numbers 6:24–26).

Think about who in this world would show you love and compassion like Jesus did. If you treated someone here on earth as you act toward God—actively rebelling, taking control at various times, and doing everything opposite of His good advice—no one would want to forgive you. Thankfully, though, God is a merciful and just God (Exodus 34:6–7). Without Him in this world, there would be all kinds of evil, and no one would forgive anyone. Without Jesus's death, we would deserve nothing in heaven. But thank God for His grace of salvation.

Prayer

Thank You, most gracious Father, for all that You do in my life and all that You will do. Thank You for sending Your Son and for dying a death I should have died. I pray that I may be able to feel Your love more often and not worry about how earthly people view me. Open my eyes and soften my heart so that I may see You and all your glory. Father, help me not fall in the enemy's trap of feeling unworthy. For I know that Your grace forgives me of all my sins. I pray this all in Jesus's name. Amen.

Application & Reflection

What did you learn from this lesson? How can you apply it to your life and others?

_____

_____

_____

_____

WALK BY FAITH, NOT BY SIGHT

If you are always dependent on what you see naturally, then you will never see what God has for you. You will constantly be looking at your most current situation, which in turn, can distract you from God (John 6:63 AMP). God may allow obstacles in your life to grab your attention. Obstacles will make you stop and seriously examine a situation, and you will have one of two options to choose from. You can be independent and rely on your own understanding, or you can humble yourself and rely on God's wisdom and guidance (Proverbs 3:5–6).

What we see in life can get us in trouble because we may easily forget that what we are seeing is a result of the battle taking place that we do not see (Ephesians 6:12). We must be conscious of what is truly going on around us. For God says if we rely on our flesh for strength, we are cursed (Jeremiah 17:5–9). What do you do when you cannot see what the future holds? Do you allow reality to set in, give up, or do you keep going? Who will you rely on, friends, family, or God? Only God can lead you to your victory. During such uncertainty, be still and listen to God as you talk with Him. For you need to walk by faith and not by sight (2 Corinthians 5:7). When you have uncertainty in your life, God may be trying to make your faith stronger and help you grow spiritually further in Him by moving you away from the elementary teachings about Christ (Hebrews 6:1–3; Luke 17:5).

When God is in the mix, your greatest victory typically comes when you cannot see the next step and have to trust Him. You can do more without your earthly understanding than you can with it because what you perceive can be deceiving. When you do not consult God, you are basically saying you do not need Him for a situation. How prideful does that sound? You may not be aware of it, but in doing so, you are declaring that you will be your own god in that situation because you are making a statement that your wisdom and knowledge are greater than the Creator's. So remember, always walk in the spirit and not by the flesh, and do not let your eyes deceive you (Galatians 5:16–18, 24–25).

Prayer

God, You are so mighty and wonderful. I am so thankful that You became a man in Jesus Christ and died for my sins so that I may approach Your throne. Father, thank You for all the trials and tribulations that come my way. For I know that suffering produces perseverance; perseverance, character; and character, hope. So through the hard times, when I do not know what to do, remind me, God, to trust Your Word and not to lean on my own understanding. Thank You for mercy during the times I am stubborn and try to figure things out on my own. Lord, help me to trust You. I pray this all in Jesus's name. Amen.

Application & Reflection

What did you learn from this lesson? How can you apply it to your life and others?

_____

_____

_____

_____

ABOVE ALL, SEEK GOD

Have you ever been so busy and begin to feel like the weight of the world is slowly piling on your shoulders? It is very easy to let yourself become distracted with the things that "must" get done. When this happens, you might feel a heaviness on you and start to feel like you are in desperate need of saving. You are in the right place when you have a desperation for God (Psalm 42:1–2). Worship and prayer can help you overcome this feeling. Worship and prayer are really all about growing in relationship with God and experiencing the love He has for you.

God is always at work with you. And sometimes you may want to question God about how He is developing your character. Be careful to question God, though. The biblical character Job did this, and God quickly showed Job how little he knew about this world and God's plan for it all (Job 38:4–7).

Since you are limited in knowing what God is doing for you, consider shouting out some praises in excitement for what God is going to do in your life. This ultimately shows that you trust the direction for your life that God will guide you on (Psalm 66:1–4).

When you are having a hard time in life and struggling with problems, what should you do? You should seek God by giving Him praise and worship (Psalm 27:8)! When you do this, you are showing God that you need Him by acknowledging He is supreme to all other things, including yourself. In doing so, God will give you an overwhelming peace (Psalm 91). Thus, you are allowing God to rule over your emotions, and you shall then overcome negative emotions with joy and ease (James 4:7–8; Romans 16:20).

What happens when you make yourself vulnerable during worship (Psalms 69:1–15; 145:14–20)? You are showing your ultimate and utter dependence on Him. This takes place as you enter God's presence by giving Him the glory He deserves by praising Him with all admiration, having your mind centered only on Him (Psalm 145:1–13).

If you've lost your motivation to worship God, you have lost your dependence on God. You then go off of your own understanding because you are now dependent on yourself (Luke 4:8; Colossians 3:16; Hebrews 13:15). If you do not know God, you cannot understand love (1 John 4:7–12). If you do not understand love, you will not feel a need for grace and mercy. If you do not feel a need for grace and mercy, you will not live in humility. If you do not live in humility, you will lose your passion to worship.

To worship fully means to praise God His way, not the way you feel you should praise Him (1 Chronicles 16:7–15, 23–36). Praising God in every circumstance is always the first step to personal victory. In short, praise God always, and stay in His mighty presence by worshipping His great name.

Prayer

Lord, You are amazing and glorious. Thank You for grace and for forgiving me of all my sins. Thank You for becoming a man and dying a death I should have died. What somber life I would have without You. Father, when I have given up, come to fear what I cannot explain, or when my anxious thoughts consume me, help me praise You. Give me a thirst to want to seek after Your face. Never let me get to the point where I feel I can depend on myself. I pray this all in Jesus's name. Amen.

Application & Reflection

What did you learn from this lesson? How can you apply it to your life and others?

_____

_____

_____

_____

PRAISE AND WORSHIP

When it comes to worshipping God, we cannot be in a hurry. When you are giving God praise through worshipping, it is a time of nearness between Him and you, even if others are around. It is a time to humble yourself because you are glorifying something bigger than yourself (Hebrews 12:28). A thought to consider: Why would you want to hurry through worshipping God, who allows you to experience His love and peace?

Praise and worship, or praising God through worship, is all about God and how you can glorify Him (Psalm 100:1–4). You should never make it about yourself. This happens when the sole reason for worshipping God is for you to receive some sort of blessing from Him. For if you do this, you are seeking after God's hand and not His face. It is all about the intention of your heart.

The whole point of singing praise and worship songs is literally to praise God through worship (Psalm 117:1–2). While doing so, you are exalting God. It's like you are saying, "Thank You," and showing God you need Him (Psalm 95:6–7). So sing songs of praise and do it for God. And do it His way, as it says to in the Bible (Psalms 95:1–5; 150:1–6). This is when the Holy Spirit will overcome you, and things will begin to move and change in your life and soul. For God is a good God and will help you as you give Him your whole heart in worship.

Prayer

Lord, I humbly come before You, giving thanks to all You have done in my life. Thank You for always coming through for me when I need it. Thank You for being the solid rock I can stand on. I ask that You help me to be conscious when I approach Your throne to give You praise. Let me not come expecting a blessing from You, but rather to exalt Your name knowing that You will not abandon me. For I know that Your plans are to prosper me and to give me hope. I pray this all in Jesus's name. Amen.

Application & Reflection

What did you learn from this lesson? How can you apply it to your life and others?

_____

_____

_____

_____

HERE TO HELP OTHERS

L ook at life as you are here to help people. If there is a stranded hiker in desperate help, a rescuer comes with a rope to pull the hiker up. Well look at it like this. Jesus is the rescuer, the sturdy rock that will not be moved. You are the rope, a tool that Jesus will use to save people from their own mistakes. The hiker is a person we encounter on a daily basis, a friend, family member, or anyone. As Jesus tosses the rope—you—down, He is placing it in the hiker's life. As the hiker starts to climb up the rope, the rope must withstand and keep from splitting and unraveling.

As you are a tool that Jesus will use, and just as the rope undergoes strain and pressure, you will too (John 15:18–20). While helping those lost, they may add pressure in your life by saying you should have sex, drink, do drugs, look at pornography, and anything else the world says is good (Galatians 5:19–21). If these pressures add too much stress on you, the rope, it will cause damage to the rope and begin to break, thus losing the rope and the hiker. However, Jesus, the rescuer, is holding tightly onto the rope, and it is not going anywhere. This symbolizes having a strong foundation in Christ (Matthew 7:24–27).

At certain moments it may feel like the rescuer is only making things worse. Perhaps things never go your way or a loved one just passed away. He is adding tension and stress, which makes it feel like the rope is unraveling and about to snap (Romans 5:3–5). But just at the last moment, as you continue to listen and stay in that situation for Jesus, the hiker makes it to the top, where the rescuer is.

The point is, when your situation is bad and it feels like Jesus is not there, that is when you need to hold on the tightest (Galatians 6:9). Otherwise, if you were to have given up and snapped, the hiker would have never been able to meet Jesus.

These "hikers" are going to come and go, test your faith, and much more. No matter how hard things get, never give in to the devil's temptation (James 4:7; Ephesians 6:11–18). The devil is smart; he is not going to come at you with something that you absolutely despise (2 Corinthians 11:14). No, he will simply start with a thought that can allow you to entertain doing an action. With that, it will be easier to be convinced to perform the action. Then it is just one compromise after another.

However, do not think that giving in to those thoughts is your only way out. When you are in those tough times helping people, and it seems like the life is being sucked out of you, think on those things that are pure (Philippians 4:8). For this will help you change your perspective. Additionally, Jesus will never give you more than you can handle (1 Corinthians 10:13).

Prayer

Father in heaven, I give thanks to You today. You are worthy of all praise. Lord, thank You for never letting go and for always seeing things through. In the analogy, if You were to let the rope go, the hiker and rope would be gone, and I—like the rope—would be gone if you stopped answering my prayers. So God, I ask that You help me persevere through the afflictions that may come when I help someone. Help me to build my faith up so that I may be a stronger rope or tool that You can use. I pray this all in Jesus's name. Amen.

Application & Reflection

What did you learn from this lesson? How can you apply it to your life and others?

_____

_____

_____

_____

WHERE YOU ARE GOING

Have you ever thought about where you want to be in life in ten years? What will stop you from getting there? What if it is yourself that is holding you back?

It is impossible to change when you keep doing the same thing. Do not be so attached to where you are or what you have that you do not want to let go. The biggest reason we cannot change is because we cannot let go. To get where God wants you, you must let go of yesterday's luggage, as Paul did (Philippians 3:12–16). Do not worry if you are too damaged or not good enough. God has a habit of taking the worst person and turning him or her into a miracle (1 Corinthians 1:26–30).

Failure to forgive could hold you back from where God wants you. If you cannot forgive your enemies, how can God forgive you (Matthew 6:14–15)? If you are not willing to leave behind all the hurt, pain, anger, and bitterness, you are not going to be able to make the journey with God (Ephesians 4:29–32; 5:1–2). So many people cannot see what God has for them today because they cannot forgive what happened yesterday. You cannot reach for anything new if your hands are still full of yesterday's junk. Of course, it is easier to hold onto yesterday's junk than to let it go because it is hard and typically hurts to let go of what you are attached to. God says come as you are, not stay as you are (Isaiah 1:18). He needs someone who is willing to change and move with Him (2 Timothy 2:15). He has asked for you to be willing.

This can easily be seen played out in various relationships. You may refuse to have relationships with people because you could be hanging onto hurt and bitterness from past experiences. Moreover, how you leave one place is how you will enter another. This can be expressed in various examples—relationships, a job, a school, and so on. Continuing with the subject of relationships, any new relationship does not even have a chance if you are still hanging on to what happened to you in an old one.

The Lord says to forgive. It is not about what happened to you; it is about how you can gain strength from it by surrendering the hurt to Jesus (Psalm 55:22). You cannot receive from God what you are not willing to give to someone else (Luke 6:37–38). You have to release something in order to receive something.

You decide where you are going in terms of growth in what the Lord has for you. So if you want to move past the old in your life and achieve the new that God has for you, you must let go of the old. Drop the old way of life; go to God to live and spiritually prosper (Ephesians 4:17–24).

Prayer

Father, I can become so prideful and wrapped up in my own ambitions. Thank You for Your Word that corrects and teaches me to humble myself. I pray that I will be able to humble myself and submit myself to Your good and perfect will. Place people in my life who will hold me accountable to let go of my pride and to forgive others. I ask that You change my perspective on things and to see the way You see things. I pray this all in Jesus's name. Amen.

Application & Reflection

What did you learn from this lesson? How can you apply it to your life and others?

_____

_____

_____

_____

Blessed Are the Pure in Heart

Jesus operated in a way so others could see the Father through His works. Therefore, when you do things, it should not be about you but about God and what will bring Him glory. For if you love God, you will do what He says so others may see Him through your works (Matthew 5:17).

Have you ever felt like God was telling you to do something, but you did not do it? Or that you heard something from Him but refused to accept it? Sometimes you may want to know the full story before doing something. With God, this will not always be the case. Even if you have taken all the steps necessary to gain understanding of what God has told you, there will still be a component of trusting His sovereignty.

Until you no longer need explanations for or results from whatever God is telling you, there is still room to grow in understanding obedience to Him (Proverbs 21:3; Luke 6:46; John 14:23). Your commitment to obey God can stem from your commitment to read His Word (Psalm 119:105–106). You cannot obey what you do not know. There is no magical way to get familiar with the words God has spoken to us through the Bible. It is something you must build your schedule around. Otherwise, you might not ever find time to read it (Psalm 1:1–3).

If you seek to hear God's voice without the discipline of meditating on His Word, you eventually take the risk of being deceived. Purity of the heart means to have one motive for everything you do—to let people see Jesus in you (John 3:30; Jeremiah 17:9; Proverbs 29:25; 2 Corinthians 2:14–15).

Prayer

Thank You, heavenly Father, for all that You do. Help me to be in obedience toward You for I want to see You. Father, I want to have a real relationship with You. Help me overcome evil passions I may have. Let my greatest passion be to obey You. Keep my heart and mind pure and set on You. I pray this all in Jesus's name. Amen.

Application & Reflection

What did you learn from this lesson? How can you apply it to your life and others?

_____

_____

_____

_____

THE IMPORTANCE OF FORGIVENESS

I have talked about forgiving others a couple of times now. Why? This is a very important concept that can really hinder your walk with Christ if it is not settled. Forgiveness is the foundation of our faith. It began when God the Father sent His Son to die for us so that we may be forgiven and accepted into relationship with God, the Father (John 3:16–17). So if we are not walking in forgiveness, then we are not living as Christ did (Matthew 6:14–15).

Forgiveness is not just something you do. It is a mindset you should live by. When you forgive people, you are showing that God is in control of your life because you are obeying what He asks of you (Mark 11:25; Ephesians 4:32). This is so because you are yielding the triggered emotions to God by releasing the person, through forgiveness, from any perceived justification owed to you from that person.

To forgive is to let go of the control of your life (Romans 12:19; Colossians 3:12–13). If you do not forgive, you are letting your emotions consume and control you (Colossians 3:8; Proverbs 19:11; 2 Corinthians 2:10–11). So if that does happen, you are telling God you know how best to handle your hurt. Therefore, making you in control of your life and needing to forgive in order to release the control of your life over to God.

The core temptation not to forgive is not hatred, greed, or lust.

It is offense. Allowing an offense to take hold in your heart can lead to wanting to get even and manifest in hatred or bitterness, thus, allowing selfish ambition to exist. This creates nothing but disorder (James 3:16). To seek revenge is an ambition that is focused only on yourself. Instead of this, you need to be eager to maintain unity among others (Ephesians 4:2–3). If you find this hard, then ask God to heal and change your heart so that you may display His grace and love (1 Corinthians 13:1–7).

When you allow resentment, hurt, or offense to fester within, you have a greater potential of becoming numb to any future hurt (Hebrews 12:15 AMP). So that past hurt can overcome you without realizing it. At that point, the hurt can easily become an identity of yours that is contrary to who God says you are (1 Peter 2:9; John 1:12). When offense is not dealt with, it can lead to dishonesty. This can be seen by being dishonest to yourself and others about your feelings, and potentially becoming dishonest to God due to hiding the hurt. In turn, this can cause you to deny the trust in God that He will heal you.

A great way to be able to forgive is to worship and pray to God. Through prayer and worship, you will experience a peace come over you that surpasses all understanding (Philippians 4:7). This allows you not to focus on whatever the hurt is but allow you to confess your sins without distractions. And God will forgive and purify you (1 John 1:9).

Once you have repented of the unforgiveness and submitted your burdens to Christ, it is time to forgive the person who hurt you (Luke 17:3–4; Colossians 3:13–14). So if you have any root of hurt or unforgiveness, ask God to remove it from your life so that you may continue forward in Christ.

Prayer

Father in heaven, thank You for first loving and forgiving me. Thank You for sending Your Son to die for me. I ask that You expose any unforgiveness in my heart. If I have been unforgiving, please forgive me and show me, so I may go and forgive the person who hurt me. Help me release all my troubles to You. Let my identity not be one of hurt but of ultimate healing in You. Guide me to live all my days filled with love. I pray this all in Jesus's name. Amen.

Application & Reflection

What did you learn from this lesson? How can you apply it to your life and others?

_____

_____

_____

_____

THE REWARD OF ENDURING

H ave you ever wondered, *What's the point to all this?* Simply put, it is to become more like Jesus Christ every day and to make His name known. Sometimes, though, becoming more Christlike can seem like a struggle. That is because the process of denying your fleshly desires, becoming more like Christ, is contrary to what you will naturally like (Luke 9:23). Often this is not an enjoyable process. The devil can try and make it seem God has abandoned you, but this is a lie (Deuteronomy 31:8).

We as humans go through so much, and you may pray to God yet feel like you are struggling to hang on. You may pray for days, weeks, maybe even years but still hear or feel nothing from God. You must not give up and always push forward. Continue to deepen your relationship with God. You have this right as a child of God (2 Corinthians 6:18).

It is in the troubled times that you will grow most with God if you allow the relationship to develop (2 Peter 3:18). There is a good seed constantly being sown into your life. Do not let the good seed—the Truth, God's Word—go to waste by falling into life's temptations (Luke 8:13). For this will steal your joy and cause you to fall away from the Father. There may be many people around you trying to counsel you. Do not let these people choke out your faith by having you worrying and chasing the riches and pleasures of life (Luke 8:14). However, do let your soul be a place where God's Word can flourish. Have your mind set on things above (Colossians 3:2). When you do, you will see results in your situation, and you will persevere (Luke 8:15)! For when you persevere, you develop a godly character that will endure all trials (Romans 8:3–5).

Even though it may feel like you are about to fall apart and break down, do not give up! When you are feeling like this, you are growing on the inside; your faith is growing stronger (2 Corinthians 4:16–17). Remember that various struggles have no power or control over you. The battle is already won in Christ Jesus. All you have to do is claim your victory through Jesus, and you will overcome the world (John 16:33). Do not fret because God will not forsake you. He will always come through and bless you.

Prayer

Father in heaven, I thank You for calling me Your child. I thank You for sacrificing Your Son, Jesus, so that I may be in a relationship with You. I ask that You cleanse my soul, remove all the sin in my life so that Your spirit may shine through me. Father, give me the strength and desire to rely on You in my times of need. Thank You for growing my faith and helping me to deny myself always so that You may be glorified. I pray this all in Jesus's name. Amen.

Application & Reflection

What did you learn from this lesson? How can you apply it to your life and others?

_____

_____

_____

_____

ALL WE NEED

The blood of Jesus Christ is all you need. Plain and simple. Think about Jesus and His character. His love for humanity was and is unmatchable. When you accept Jesus as your Lord and Savior, you are transformed from the inside out, and you are then empowered to live like Jesus. You can love others as He did, and you can know what love is because you can be confident that God is love (1 John 4:16).

If you walk with Jesus in love and righteousness and submit to His Lordship, what else do you really need? Houses, clothes, cars, and food are all very nice and needed, but think about it. People in third world countries have little to nothing, yet they will praise God with all their hearts. God provides food for the birds, so why should you worry? Worrying will not add anything to your life (Matthew 6:25–33).

You may be on the verge of losing everything, may it be physically, mentally, relationship-wise, or material things (1 John 2:17). You will lose these things when you pass from the earth, so why chase after them as if they bring fulfillment and life? In fact, what you should be working toward is offering yourself to God as a living sacrifice, submitting your will and desires to God, accepting His Lordship (Romans 12:1–2). For when you yield to God's will in your life, good things will come to you (Job 22:21–25). When you submit to His will for you, your heart will become focused on righteousness, and He will bring you the desires of your heart (Psalm 37:4).

He is so kind and cares for you so greatly that He sent His Son to die for your sins so that you may be able to be in a relationship with Him (John 3:16). Let that sink in. "In this is love, not that we loved God, but that He loved us and sent His Son to be the propitiation for our sins" (1 John 4:10). So what do you need again? Nothing but Jesus. His blood paid for all the evil in your soul and spirit. Jesus redeemed you.

When things get bad, I see that as a time to cry out to God, to press in, and to discover how good God is (Psalm 145:18). So trust in Him through the good and the bad. God makes the best of things out of the worst of situations.

Prayer

I seek after Your righteousness and make You the priority in my life. I ask that You show Your blessings and power in my life. Let my life be a living sacrifice for You, and let others see You in all my deeds. I have faith that as I keep Your commandments and do the things that bring You honor, I will receive what I ask from You because it is to bring You honor. Thank You, Lord, for being a man of Your word. I pray this all in Jesus's name. Amen.

Application & Reflection

What did you learn from this lesson? How can you apply it to your life and others?

_____

_____

_____

_____

LIFESTYLE

What kind of lifestyle are you living? Are you living one that exemplifies God, one that is pursuing righteousness? On the outside, you could very easily be performing the works of a Christian or even a "good person." However, what are your real motives? Are you trying to earn your salvation, which is moralism, or are you living a life that has resulted in a nature change because you understand you do nothing to earn God's grace (Ephesians 2:8)?

This world pushes for you to live an unholy lifestyle. However, you cannot just blame it all on this decaying world. You must also take ownership of your wrongdoings. But how are you containing those wrongdoings? Is it by covering your motives and sin with "good" moral behavior, thus changing external behavior but never fixing the root issue? If it is by moralism, the heart will eventually revert to its original state, sin.

If you are a Christian and have God's nature, then you will have an odd feeling about evil. This is because you now have a righteous nature and the Holy Spirit dwelling within you, so you will feel repelled by the evil around you (1 Corinthians 6:19–20). When you feel this way, do not ignore it because the Holy Spirit is telling you not to do or be around that particular thing (James 4:17). If you do ignore the Holy Spirit and begin to notice you do not have the feeling that was urging you to stay away, it is likely from accepting the evil around you and have become numb to it (Ephesians 4:30). God cannot be in the same place as sin (Isaiah 59:1–3). There is no room for sin and God. One must only serve one master (Matthew 6:24). Allow the peace of God to guard your heart (Philippians 4:7).

Alternatively, if you have not accepted the good news of Jesus Christ and not had a nature change, then you might notice yourself speaking things that are corrupting your soul. For out of your heart can come evil thoughts (Matthew 15:18–19). What you say matters because what you say defines you. Furthermore, if you have or have not accepted Jesus as your Lord and Savior and find yourself speaking death and negativity over your life and your situations, you should stop. Speaking negatively brings the worst into every situation (Proverbs 18:21; 13:2). Start speaking life, and once you do, watch your life change around. So speak to the problem in a positive way, and you will notice your thoughts and feelings align with the positive words (Proverbs 16:24).

Prayer

God, I ask that You reveal to me if I truly have had a nature change. Show me if my actions to serve You have been moralistic like the Pharisees, or if my will is bent to Your will. Holy Spirit, please continue to guide and correct me as I near the edge of good and evil. Help me to seek always after the righteousness of God. I pray this all in Jesus's name. Amen.

Application & Reflection

What did you learn from this lesson? How can you apply it to your life and others?

_____

_____

_____

_____

NO LONGER

A relationship with Jesus Christ. What is that like? Is it where we are rewarded for only the good that we do? Perhaps it is where we get close to Him, and then He just rips the carpet out from under us and leaves us there alone. No! None of these are correct.

Experiencing a relationship with Jesus is like no other experience on earth (1 John 3:1). Imagine doing the most unimaginable thing possible to the one you love. Now imagine that person embracing you with open arms and with forgiveness instead of turning away from you. This is exactly what God does because He wishes for you to live (Ezekiel 18:31–32). That is what it is like to have a relationship with Christ.

You are no longer alone and forgotten (Jeremiah 29:11). When everyone you love turns their backs on you, there is God waiting for you (Psalm 27:10). In fact, God sends angels to fight your battles for you, so you shall never be alone again when in a relationship with Him (Psalm 34:7).

Believing in God and accepting His Son, Jesus, as your Lord and Savior will give you the most hope you can think of. This is not because you are simply forgetting about your troubles. Rather, you face them by surrendering them to a Higher Power (Psalms 55:22; 37:5). You accept the fact that it is something out of your control. For the gospel of Jesus Christ is good news (Luke 4:17–21, 43). It is that God became man through Jesus, lived the life we should have lived, and died in our place; we should have died. He rose three days later, proving He is the Son of God. By so doing, He offers the gift of salvation and forgiveness of sins to everyone who repents and believes in Him (John 1:14; Romans 4:25; John 3:16).

This does not mean to just stop your life, go sit in a corner, and say, "God has it." For the Bible says faith without works is dead (Romans 10:13–15; James 2:14–26). A relationship with Christ means to have open communication with Him, a prayer life, and one that consists of more than just, "Gimme, gimme." It should be one that thanks Him for everything in your life because everything you have and that happens to you is all to guide you into experiencing the love of the heavenly Father. In all situations, God works for the good of those who love Him (Romans 8:28).

A relationship with Christ means to give honor where honor is due. He is the Creator of everything, so worship Him by thanking and worshipping Him in all that you do. So what does it mean to be in a relationship with Jesus? It means to allow the gospel of Jesus Christ to produce in you love, joy, peace, patience, kindness, goodness, faithfulness, gentleness, and self-control (Galatians 5:22).

Prayer

Jesus, I repent from all known sins in my life. I turn away from continuing to practice sin. I declare that You are my Lord and Savior. I trust in Your ways for my life. I will no longer live to my own desires. God, empower me with the Holy Spirit to be able to live out all that You have called me to, and to be able to share the gospel of Jesus Christ. Thank You for loving me and for wanting me to experience Your love. I pray this all in Jesus's name. Amen.

Application & Reflection

What did you learn from this lesson? How can you apply it to your life and others?

_____

_____

_____

_____

BEAUTIFUL EXCHANGE

Have you ever felt distant from God? It is reasonable to say that most people have felt this way at some point in their lives. However, God is always right there with you! He is never too far or out of reach (Acts 17:27).

In fact, it is your sin that separates you from God. Your sin hides you from God, making it seem as though He has left you when it is, indeed, the other way around (Isaiah 59:1–2). Moreover, God is always giving you a way out from your own temptation (James 1:13–15; 1 Corinthians 10:13). He is always fighting for you and will not let anything happen to His children (Exodus 14:14). Keep in mind your battle is not a fight of flesh and blood but against evil spiritual forces (Ephesians 6:12).

After reading through God's Word, it seems as though there is nothing you can do by your own works to shorten the separation between you and Him. In reality, there is absolutely nothing you can do by your own strength. It is only by God's grace to forgive and purify you that you can draw near to Him (1 John 1:9). That grace and mercy were given to you when Jesus Christ paid the wages due for your sins (John 14:6; Romans 6:23). For it is because of one man's disobedience—the first of mankind—that you suffer and do not experience a closeness with your heavenly Father. But through the obedience of one man—Jesus—you are made righteous and can have a close relationship with God (Romans 5:19). Because of humankind being unholy and God being wonderfully holy, an exchange had to be made. Jesus died for your wrongdoings, your evilness, so that you could once again be in a close relationship with God (1 John 2:2; Hebrews 9:12; 1 Timothy 2:5).

Once you have accepted Jesus as your Lord and Savior, you soon realize how joyful, peaceful, and merciful it is to have a relationship with the Lord. As you grow in your relationship with Christ, you may at times feel distant from God. This should be an indicator to examine your life and see if there are any unconfessed sin patterns (Proverbs 28:13; Psalm 66:18). If any are found, let the gospel of Jesus Christ change your heart in that area. Do not try to correct it by performing religious works (Ephesians 2:8–9; Galatians 3:2–14). As you do so, remember that as followers of Christ, empowered by the Holy Spirit, we have the power to overcome sin (Galatians 5:16).

Prayer

Father in heaven, I thank You and give You praise for thinking so much of me that You would come down to earth, become a man, and die for my sins so we can once again be in a close relationship. I was lost and insecure, but You were there for me. I ask that the Holy Spirit refresh me and give me the empowerment to overcome all kinds of temptation. Let me see You in everything I do. I pray this all in Jesus's name. Amen.

Application & Reflection

What did you learn from this lesson? How can you apply it to your life and others?

_____

_____

_____

_____

TRUST IN HIS LOVE

L ove. Why do so many people say they love this and love that? The word "love" seems to have lost its value over time. The Bible says love is patient, kind, does not envy, does not boast, is not proud, does not dishonor others, is not self-seeking, is not easily angered, keeps no record of wrongs, does not delight in evil but rejoices with the truth, always protects, always trusts, always hopes, and always perseveres (1 Corinthians 13:4–7).

The Bible is clear how love should be expressed. Showing love to a person is something we are commanded to do (1 Peter 4:8). It may at times be hard to do, but it is doable. This is when accepting Jesus as Lord and Savior comes in handy because the Holy Spirit empowers you to love others the way God intended you to.

The Bible is also clear that expressing or showing godly love will overcome a multitude of sins (1 Peter 4:8). Imagine someone who is consumed with wickedness or mental distress. All you have to do to help the individual is to humble yourself and allow the Holy Spirit to work through you to show love to him or her. God's love should be a foundation in your life (1 John 4:7–11). If you build your entire life around God's great love, like that expressed in Jeremiah 31:3, you will form biblical characteristics and be able not to find fault in others nor anger easily. So when arguments occur, you will be able to avoid getting wrapped up in the moment and let your emotions control you. You will be empowered to show love such as God does to all humanity (Psalm 86:15).

Most important, you must first love God because if you do not show love to the One who created you, how can you show love to others (1 John 4:19–21)? His love is the foundation for us to love others. If we do not love the One who created us, then we cannot love ourselves, and thus, we will not be able to show love to others (1 John 4:12–17).

A situation may arise that will make you feel out of control. If and when that day comes, remember that responding in anger and hatred will only create conflict. But love will cover all wrongdoings (Proverbs 10:12). Examine your life and heart every day. Ask yourself, "Am I expressing godly love that the Bible outlines?"

Prayer

Jesus, I thank You for willingly sacrificing Yourself to die for my sin, something I should have paid for. You have extinguished the debt I owed to God. Because of this, I can now know and experience the love God has for me. I ask that the Holy Spirit invade every part of my soul and remove any hatred I have toward my fellow brothers and sisters in Christ. Help and empower me, God, to demonstrate the love You showed to humanity through Jesus. I pray this all in Jesus's name. Amen.

Application & Reflection

What did you learn from this lesson? How can you apply it to your life and others?

_____

_____

_____

_____

PERSEVERE UNDER TRIAL

Have you ever felt like quitting a task, school, or even life? Whatever it may be, I am sure most people at some point in their lives wanted to quit something. However, God's Word tells you to do the opposite. It actually encourages you to persevere in faith, and by doing so, God blesses you (James 1:12).

God surely has called His people to be set apart from the culture around them (Leviticus 20:26; 1 Peter 2:9). Persevering in faith through trials can look like many things. Maybe it is through a financial hardship, an illness, or a relationship. Whatever the situation, while going through a trial, there is almost always something tempting you that is averse to the Word of God.

Be careful about who or what you put the blame on for tempting you. Remember, God will never put you in a situation where He is tempting you (James 1:13–15). You actually put yourself in situations like that due to your own evil desires. Once you give in to your evil desire, that allows the devil to have legal rights to that area of your soul; you allowed sin to be birthed there through acting on an evil desire (1 John 3:4–10; 1 Peter 5:8–9). Because of the sin that has been birthed, it will continue to grow if practiced and not dealt with, and you will be consumed by that practiced sin. Furthermore, God, in His lovingkindness, will never leave you alone in those tempting situations (Isaiah 41:10; 1 Corinthians 10:13).

The real issue is whether you trust that God loves you enough to get you through any situation. If you do not trust Him, you will ultimately give in to the temptation you are facing because you will not see or believe how God will come through for you. Nevertheless, all of God's answers to His promises is, "Yes" (2 Corinthians 1:20; Romans 4:21). So when temptation is around you, and it seems like it is easier to quit, persevere because the pressure will produce faith and character in you (Romans 5:3–5; James 1:2–4; 1 Peter 4:12–13).

Prayer

Jesus, You are worthy of all praise. I sing praises to Your name and give You honor. Thank You for enduring every kind of temptation and overcoming them because now I have power through the Holy Spirit to do the same. Lord, strengthen my discernment so I may not get caught in the devil's trap, and give me wisdom to not put myself in tempting situations. Make known to me what evil desires are in my heart leading to temptation so that I might surrender them to You. I proclaim that I trust You and that I want to do Your will here on earth as it is in heaven. I pray this all in Jesus's name. Amen.

Application & Reflection

What did you learn from this lesson? How can you apply it to your life and others?

_____

_____

_____

_____

YOU ARE ENOUGH

You may be crying out to God, "I am torn in many ways." Maybe you felt as though you were on top of the world, but then you were shown where you were wrong (Isaiah 43:18–19). Is your faith weak? Were you wrong all this time about having faith in God (Psalm 51:10)? Do you ever ask why you should continue to try to do what God's Word says? Perhaps you feel insignificant in this large world and in the grander plan God has configured. Will you ever be able to fulfill the role God has given you? Moreover, maybe you ask yourself, "Am I that messed up of a person that I cannot even walk in what You, God, have called me to do and be?"

God's grace covers your sins, every last one of them (2 Corinthians 12:9). You surely do not have all the answers to your problems. However, all you need is to humble yourself and trust Him; He is all you need (2 Peter 1:3; Jeremiah 33:3). You may not feel it now, but you must continue to proclaim God's Word over your life. God prevails every time (Isaiah 14:24; Job 42:2; Exodus 14:14). Experiences with God are not of this world and cannot be duplicated (Exodus 33:14; Joshua 1:9; Psalm 27:4). So continue to tell yourself to keep relying on God and to keep moving forward (Psalm 20:7; Jeremiah 29:13).

Though you may feel numb to God's presence in the middle of conflict and turmoil, or feel as though you are not ready for what He has called you to do, know this: He wishes only to be with and comfort you so He can take away any and all anguish in your soul

(Psalm 46:1–3; John 16:22; Matthew 5:4; 2 Corinthians 1:3–4). So what must you do? You must continue to tell yourself that God is indeed enough and all you need (Psalm 16:5–11; Matthew 6:33).

Prayer

Lord, I want to let go of my soul and everything that I am holding onto. I ask that I will be emptied and that You will be the only thing that fills me. Thank You for being so merciful and ever-present in my time of need. You never leave me or forsake me. Thank You for being enough for me. Help me, oh God, for my spirit to cry out to You and proclaim, "It is well with my soul." I pray this all in Jesus's name. Amen.

Application & Reflection

What did you learn from this lesson? How can you apply it to your life and others?

_____

_____

_____

_____

CONTROLLING YOUR MIND AND YOUR ACTIONS

Have you ever had a thought or desire that seemed harmless, but in retrospect, it was truly evil and contrary to God's nature (Jeremiah 17:9)? Did you act on that thought or desire (James 1:15)? Once you act on that desire, it entangles you, and that desire will seem to become easier and easier to do. Or another way to say it is that you become numb to that sin (Hebrews 12:1; 1 Timothy 4:1–2).

The way to stop negative thoughts from ever becoming actions is to take them captive by literally saying, "I take the thought captive in the name of Jesus" (2 Corinthians 10:5). From there, you find scriptures that nullify that evil and speak them aloud. Make that scripture a declaration for your life (John 6:63; Hebrews 4:12). You say things audibly, even if to yourself, because your words have power (Proverbs 18:21; 12:14; Matthew 12:37; James 3:3–6).

The Bible also tells us to turn away from our youthful lust (2 Timothy 2:22). No matter when this lust developed, there is a season of ignorance and youthfulness, the time in life before enlightenment that Jesus is Lord. There is also a time to develop a real love for people, which requires you to respect all people in all situations. Once you become saved, you are no longer ignorant of your actions, and you are held to a higher standard (1 Peter 1:14).

Not conforming to your evil desires allows you to respect others. This starts by taking your thoughts captive in the name of Jesus so that they do not become your actions (Romans 12:2). So controlling your actions starts with controlling your thoughts.

Prayer

Lord, there are many things I am unaware of. Help me understand the darkest parts of my heart so that I may understand the root of my thoughts and actions. Holy Spirit, empower me to overcome the lustful thoughts of my youth. Lord, develop me to become mature in knowledge and action. Knowledge concerning You and my actions when it comes to Your Word. Thank You for making me exactly how You planned, and thank You for showing me where I have accepted lies about myself. I pray this all in Jesus's name. Amen.

Application & Reflection

What did you learn from this lesson? How can you apply it to your life and others?

_____

_____

_____

_____

DESPAIR: A TRAP

I magine this, you pray, fast, and seek godly counsel. And you strongly believe that a certain situation has to be of God's will. What would you do if that situation came true, but then it all crumbles, and the situation begins to look more like a failure? Would you trust God's sovereignty and take your thoughts captive? Or would you allow yourself to spiral into despair?

Despair can be caused by various situations. For example, God may excel you to the top, and then you fall into what feels like a pit of disappointment. Although God still takes care of you, it is easy to look at your current situation and say, "But God, I thought I was meant for more." You have to be careful of falling victim to this because you can quickly lose sight of Him (Deuteronomy 8:11–14; 16–18). You must always remind yourself that God feeds the birds, so He shall take care of you, who He carefully and thoughtfully designed (Matthew 6:26–34; Psalm 139:13–14). Also remember that His ways are not your ways, and His thoughts are higher than your thoughts (Isaiah 55:8–9). So be careful not to get upset if He is directing your life in a different direction than you think it should go.

Your response to situations like this is what will grow you spiritually. Press into the Lord. Search the scriptures to see what He says to do in situations like this. Remind yourself of all that the Lord has brought you through. Habakkuk 3:17–18 shows exactly what you should do when in your life it feels appropriate to be miserable and dismayed. Even if nothing is going according to plan, you should rejoice in the Lord and be joyful because God is your Savior. He will always come to the rescue (Ezekiel 34:11–12).

Situations can look dreadful and miserable. Things can go from good to bad and from bad to worse in a heartbeat. As you adjust to the challenges that life throws at you, it is imperative to remind yourself that the God of the universe will take care of you, and the Holy Spirit will always comfort you (Romans 15:13).

Prayer

Father in heaven, You are so gracious and merciful. I repent for the times I am unfaithful and doubt Your ways. I am thankful that You are faithful and never go back on Your Word. I ask that You fill me with joy. With a joy that overflows and that is contagious to others. Give me opportunities to share why I am joyful in such bad times, opportunities to share the gospel. Thank You, Father, for delivering me from the devil's schemes. I pray this all in Jesus's name. Amen.

Application & Reflection

What did you learn from this lesson? How can you apply it to your life and others?

_____

_____

_____

_____